Original title:
Gravitational Guffaws

Copyright © 2025 Creative Arts Management OÜ
All rights reserved.

Author: Eleanor Prescott
ISBN HARDBACK: 978-1-80567-780-2
ISBN PAPERBACK: 978-1-80567-901-1

Whirlwind Witty Ways

A lighthearted spin in the cosmos,
Where laughter floats like dancing prose.
Gravity's giggle on a comet's tail,
Jokes soar high, like a playful gale.

Nebulas swirl in a colorful dance,
Stars winking down, giving joy a chance.
With each bright flash, a chuckle's shared,
In this universe, humor is bared.

Planets wobble in their jovial prance,
Orbiting jokes, skipping in a trance.
One slip and fall, a celestial slip,
Cosmic laughter in a starry trip.

Asteroids chuckle on their rocky ride,
Shooting through space with humorous pride.
As black holes laugh, pulling at the seams,
In this wild orbit, we dance in dreams.

Cosmic Clowning

In the circus of space, where comets bark,
Jupiters juggle while Saturns embark.
Galaxies giggle in spiraled delight,
As stars play tag in the velvety night.

A moonbeam slips on a path made of light,
Falling to Earth in a playful fright.
Laughter erupts like a supernova's glow,
Echoing far in the cosmic show.

Quasars wink with a mischievous flair,
As black holes spin tales, if you dare.
In this vastness, where whimsy reigns,
Even the void can't hold back the gains.

So come take a ride on this celestial train,
Where humor and joy are no longer plain.
Here, laughter's the spark that ignites our souls,
In cosmic clowning, we find our roles.

Fractured Frolics

A puppy jumped and soared too high,
It landed in a pizza pie.
With cheese upon its little nose,
It grinned wide, like a clown in prose.

A cat in boots was on a roll,
Chasing shadows, losing control.
With every leap, it did a spin,
In a dance, it forgot to win.

Comedic Cosmos

Stars giggle in the night so bright,
As planets trip in silly flight.
A comet sneezes, dust goes high,
While moons chase tails across the sky.

Galaxies whirl in a jitterbug,
While meteors dance a cosmic shrug.
Black holes chuckle, pulling things in,
Creating jokes with every spin.

Echoes of Exuberance

Laughter echoes through the air,
As ducks wear bowties without a care.
A squirrel slipped on a banana peel,
And the trees shook with a hearty squeal.

Frogs in hats sing songs of cheer,
While butterflies twirl, spreading good cheer.
The sun winks down at the scene below,
As nature's jesters put on a show.

Stellar Smirks

A rocket ship with a silly grin,
Did cartwheels in the void's great din.
It shouted joy, and what a sight,
As aliens joined in on the flight.

Saturn's rings danced to a tune,
With cosmic cheers that made hearts swoon.
Even black holes find time to play,
In the universe's funny ballet.

Laughter in Zero Gravity

In outer space, we float and glide,
Our laughter echoes, no place to hide.
A ticklish comet zipped right by,
We giggled hard, then watched it fly.

With wobbly steps, we dance around,
A cosmic jig, a silly sound.
Our snacks drift close, a tasty tease,
We munch on air, and float with ease.

The Weight of Whimsy

A plump little planet rolls on by,
Chasing stars, it wonders why.
It laughs and giggles, round and stout,
With every spin, it wiggles out.

Its moons, they chase like playful pups,
As they leap and bound, they giggle up.
In gravity's grip, they play a game,
And every bounce sounds just the same.

Celestial Shenanigans

Among the stars, a prankster glows,
It whispers jokes that only cosmos knows.
Galaxies spin in fits of cheer,
As laughter rings from ear to ear.

A black hole swirled with silly sights,
Sucking in giggles, with all its might.
While asteroids tumble with a clatter,
They tumble forth, then burst in laughter.

Orbiting Humor

This moon spins round in joyful tunes,
Playing tag with bright marooned balloons.
It twirls and sways, a playful sight,
Reflecting laughter in the night.

In solar winds, the jokes take flight,
As planets giggle, day and night.
Through cosmic dust and starry beams,
They share the silliest of dreams.

Saturn's Sassy Laughter

In rings of gold, she twirls with glee,
Her moons all chuckle, can't you see?
With every spin, a giggle spills,
A cosmic dance that tickles thrills.

The stars all wink, up high they gleam,
While comets rush with silly dreams.
Laughter echoes through the night,
As Saturn sings of pure delight.

Interstellar Improv

In the vast void, a joke's unfurled,
A supernova's punchline swirled.
Galactic jesters take the stage,
With witty quips, they'll never age.

Planets nod in rhythmic fun,
While stardust showers, laughter spun.
Cosmic puns, they float around,
In this grand show, joy is found.

The Comedic Cosmos

Constellations waltz in silly twirls,
With every star, the laughter swirls.
Black holes snicker, steal the light,
As meteors dash, a playful sight.

A nebula bursts with painted cheer,
Alien antics are always near.
Superstars chuckle, sharing the jest,
In this vast space, we're truly blessed.

Joviality in Orbit

Through spirals bright, the jesters spin,
With cosmic smiles, they boldly grin.
Orbiting joy, they leap and play,
In the dance of night, come what may.

Light-years crossed in burst of glee,
A universe swayed by harmony.
Twinkling laughter fills the space,
As worlds unite in funny grace.

Jovial Journeys

On a trip to the stars, we all wore big hats,
Floating with laughter, avoiding the bats.
Spaceships went zooming, but ours lost the race,
As we tumbled and giggled, what a wild place!

Bouncing on moons made of fluffy white cheese,
We danced with the comets, a cosmic tease.
Every bad pun made us wobble and roll,
In the universe's belly, we lost all control.

Cosmic Capers

Stargazing parties with marshmallow snacks,
Aliens pranked us, and we had to relax.
We tripped over stardust, all covered in goo,
As laughter erupted, the cosmos just flew!

Asteroids playing hide and seek up in space,
Caught one in a hug; what a clumsy embrace!
Each twist and each turn brought a chuckle divine,
As we floated through giggles on a galactic line.

Moonlit Merriment

Under the moonlight, we gathered in cheer,
With jokes about gravity pulling us near.
Space squirrels with acorns made ruckus and noise,
While we chased through the night, all the girls and the boys.

A telescope wobbling led to silly sights,
We peeked at the stars in their glittery lights.
Each wink from the cosmos whispered a jest,
In the laughter-filled night, we simply felt blessed.

Gravity's Comedy Show

A stage in the sky under twinkling bright,
With planets as seats, and the stars as our lights.
Comedians telling jokes that made no sense,
While we held our sides and laughed at the expense.

A black hole cracked jokes, and it pulled us right in,
"Why did the rocket skip the gym? No spin!"
As laughter erupted, we all lost our breath,
In this cosmic cabaret, we laughed 'til we left.

Falling for Fun

In a world where giggles soar,
We tumble down, who could ask for more?
Like clowns on stilts, we twist and twirl,
Gravity's pull makes our laughter swirl.

With bouncy bumps and silly falls,
We bounce right back to heed the calls,
Of tickled ribs and cheerful yelps,
Where every stumble's a joke that helps.

Playful Orbits

Round and round the dance floor spins,
With silly steps and cheeky grins.
We sway like planets in a whirl,
As laughter rockets and joy unfurls.

Each playful move, a cosmic jest,
In this ballet of laughter, we're blessed.
Oh, let us twirl to joking tunes,
In orbits spun by our giggling moons.

Astrological Antics

Stars wink down with a wink,
As we trip over comets, who would think?
Zany patterns fill the sky,
As laughing meteors zoom by.

Constellations crack a smile,
While we laugh and dance in style.
Our silly signs in every chart,
Bring bursts of joy that warm the heart.

Laughing in the Void

In a universe where fun is free,
We float through space, just you and me.
With every gulp of cosmic air,
We guffaw and giggle without a care.

Stars shine bright with comic glee,
As we bounce on dimensions of whimsy.
In the silence where echoes play,
We laugh out loud, come what may.

Celestial Cackles

Stars twinkle with glee,
Planets dance on a spree,
Comets trail in delight,
Creating a cosmic night.

Laughter bounces off moons,
Echoes of silly tunes,
Galaxies spin with cheer,
As space tickles the sphere.

Martians giggle in fleets,
Warped jokes in rocket beats,
Asteroids chuckle and bounce,
In the void, the fun counts.

Saturn's rings spin around,
In laughter, peace is found,
The Milky Way's a stage,
For clowns of every age.

Humor on the Horizon

The sun winks in the sky,
Clouds wear a playful tie,
Wind whispers a light jest,
As laughter fills the quest.

Planets play peek-a-boo,
While the stars giggle too,
Comets twirl in delight,
Joy travels through the night.

Rockets zoom with a laugh,
Galaxies draw a path,
Meteorites crack a smile,
Making space awe worthwhile.

With humor in the stars,
And lightyears full of jars,
Each orbit holds a grin,
Let the cosmic fun begin!

Laughs from the Cosmos

Nebulas burst with glee,
While black holes sip their tea,
Pulsars crack witty puns,
As space unfolds its runs.

Planets trade funny tales,
In a dance without fails,
Asteroids roll on the floor,
Creating joy evermore.

Supernovae flash wide,
In laughter, they confide,
As time tickles the void,
All worries are destroyed.

Cosmic giggles abound,
In the starlight, they're found,
No end to the delight,
When the universe takes flight.

Snapshots of Celestial Joy

In the sky, snapshots gleam,
Where every star has a dream,
Galaxies pose with flair,
Joy reflected everywhere.

Comets strike a silly pose,
In laughter, the cosmos glows,
Astrophysics in a grin,
Where joy and light begin.

The moons share inside jokes,
As stardust giggles and pokes,
Lightyears filled with mischief,
Creating galactic relief.

Each twinkle holds a jest,
In the heavens, we're blessed,
Catch the humor that flies,
In the vast azure skies.

Cosmic Joyride

In a rocket built from cheese,
We zoom past stars with ease.
Asteroids dance, they wiggle and sway,
As comets laugh, whoosh past our way.

Space squirrels juggling cosmic nuts,
Tumble and twirl, oh what a fuss!
Planets spinning, they join in the fun,
Orbiting joy 'neath the alien sun.

Stellar Snickers

A black hole with a jolly grin,
Pulls in laughter, let the fun begin.
Galaxies giggle in spiral formation,
Creating a raucous, hilarious sensation.

Stars wink at us with twinkling glee,
As they hum tunes from a cosmic spree.
Supernovas burst with chuckling roars,
Filling the void with mirth galore.

The Gravity of Giggles

Rocket ships with rubber tires,
Zoom through space, fueled by desires.
Meteor showers tickle and tease,
While nebulae spray cosmic cheese.

With space-time bending, jokes take flight,
Ticklish wonders in the starry night.
Orbiting laughter, a celestial loop,
Spinning around this interstellar troupe.

Spacebound Chucklefest

Floating high above the earth,
A cosmic circus full of mirth.
Zany aliens with floppy hats,
Crackling jokes like nimble acrobats.

Moonbeams bouncing, laughter ignites,
In absurd dances, all feels right.
Twirling comets, a merry parade,
In this spacebound fest, joy is displayed.

Celestial Comedy Starlight

In the night sky, stars wink bright,
They dance and twirl, a joyous sight.
Black holes giggle, spinning around,
While comets play tag, oh what a sound!

Planets chuckle, each in its sway,
Jupiter's storm laughing away.
Moonbeams tickle the earth below,
As stardust sprinkles a glittery show.

Playful Pulsars

Pulsars pulse with a rhythm fun,
A cosmic joke, a race just begun.
They giggle with light, a flickering tease,
While space dust chuckles, carried by breeze.

In rings of Saturn, the laughter flows,
As tiny asteroid friends strike silly poses.
Each twinkling star shares a giggly jest,
In this vast universe, we're all truly blessed.

Galactic Giggles

Galaxies swirl in a swirling laugh,
Hitching a ride on a meteor's path.
Nebulas puff with a loud guffaw,
As they paint the dark with a brilliant draw.

Cosmic dust bunnies hop and skitter,
Why do they giggle? No one can titter.
The distant quasars join the spree,
In this cosmic circus, we're all set free.

Cosmic Chortles

Stars burst forth with a joyous shout,
Creating new worlds in a playful bout.
Asteroids laugh as they pass by,
Making comical shapes in the night sky.

Wormholes twist with a playful grin,
Inviting all brave souls to spin.
In this universe, laughter's our guide,
As we dance in space with glee and pride.

Stardust Shenanigans

In the cosmos where laughter spills,
Stars play tricks with their glittering frills.
Comets dance with a wink and a jig,
Stardust whispers, 'Come, be big!'

Planets roll with a chuckling cheer,
Spinning tales that we long to hear.
Nebulas giggle, clouds puff out tease,
Cosmic jokes float on solar breeze.

Eclipses of Amusement

When the moon steals the light in the night,
The stars blink twice, 'What a silly sight!'
Shadows laugh as the sun wears a grin,
In this cosmic comedy, joys begin.

Solar flares burst with a giggly glow,
While meteorites tumble to put on a show.
Each eclipse brings a tickle, a smile,
As laughter wraps round the void for a while.

Galactic Grins

Across the void, smiles stretch and gleam,
Stars beam brightly, quite the dream team.
Asteroids chuckle as they quietly roll,
In the dance of the cosmos, we lift our soul.

Wormholes wobble, twinkling in flight,
While galaxies shimmer with pure delight.
The universe hums a quirky tune,
Beneath the watchful gaze of the moon.

Quirky Quasars

Quasars bicker in the cosmic night,
Spouting jokes that take off in flight.
A redshift here, a giggle there,
Interstellar humor fills the air.

With twinkling eyes, they tease and play,
Lighting up dark matter in a funny way.
In their radiant glow, we see the fun,
In a universe busting with laughter, on the run.

Laughs Above the Atmosphere

In the sky, a comet zooms,
It trips on stardust, laughter blooms.
Planets giggle, stars conspire,
To create a cosmic choir.

Moonbeams twirl in silly dance,
Tickling clouds, they take a chance.
Galaxies snicker, what a sight,
As space turns silly, day and night.

Grin and Glide

Floating up, where comets slide,
A ticklish breeze, we laugh and ride.
Nebulas puff, a colorful show,
While satellites stumble in their flow.

The sun cracks jokes, in rays so bright,
Winks at Earth with pure delight.
Asteroids trip on cosmic swirls,
Spinning tales, as laughter unfurls.

Hilarity in the Heavens

Stars burst forth with gleeful light,
In the vast expanse, what a sight!
Saturn's rings, they giggle and spin,
   Jovial jests, where to begin?

A meteor sings as it flies by,
With a punchline that makes us sigh.
Laughter echoes, a joyful sound,
As the universe turns round and round.

Lunar Levity

The moon plays pranks in silver hues,
Dancing with shadows, singing the blues.
Stars throw confetti, a radiant burst,
In this playful realm, humor's first.

With a skip and a hop, they leap and bound,
Earth chuckles softly, a joyous sound.
Celestial secrets, shared with glee,
In the laughter of space, we're forever free.

Nebula Nods

In the cosmos, stars take flight,
Comets dance with pure delight.
A cosmic joke, so bright and clear,
Planets giggle, round they cheer.

With every twinkle, chuckles rise,
Galaxies wink with laughter's sighs.
Black holes yawn, a comical sight,
As stardust tumbles, so light and bright.

Spirals of Silliness

Whirls and swirls in the night sky,
Asteroids joke, they flutter by.
Jupiter jests with a merry spin,
While Saturn's rings hum a silly din.

spirals twirl in joyous play,
Nebulas giggle, come what may.
A dance of laughter, wild and free,
Cosmic clowns in a grand marquee.

The Joyous Abyss

Deep in space, where shadows dwell,
Lurks a void that giggles well.
Stars fall in, with a playful plop,
As echoing chuckles never stop.

In the depths, a cheeky grin,
Gravity pulls, let the fun begin.
Cosmic pranks from light-years away,
In the dark, let the jokes play.

Luminous Laughter

Light years echo with a roar,
Galactic gags that we adore.
Solar flares tickle the sun,
A radiant joy that's never done.

Twinkling stars with a wink and cheer,
Bringing giggles from far and near.
In the cosmos, humor's vast,
A timeless jest, a cosmic blast.

When Planets Joke

In cosmic halls where planets spin,
They whisper jokes with a cheeky grin.
Mars winks at Venus, 'You're looking round!'
While Jupiter laughs, a booming sound.

Saturn's rings are a ticklish sight,
They dance and twirl, what a funny flight!
Earth says, 'What did one star say to another?'
'You're my light, can't find a better brother!'

Ticklish Tides

Waves giggle softly on sandy shores,
Tides tickle toes, laughter soars.
The moon grins bright with a silvery beam,
While shells chime in, joining the theme.

A seagull swoops, with a clumsy dive,
Sprays water high, oh how they thrive!
Amidst the frolic, crabs do a jig,
The ocean's humor, both grand and big!

The Gravity of Humor

In a world where laughter weighs a ton,
Every joke lands like a playful pun.
With each small chuckle, we float away,
Like balloons escaping at the end of the day.

A cosmic scale measuring glee,
One joke's gravity, wild and free!
We orbit around the brightest laughs,
Making memories, our silly crafts.

Comets in Cackles

Comets streak by with gleeful trails,
Leaving behind their shimmering tales.
Each whoosh and whirl, a giggle released,
As stardust dances, the laughter increased.

With tails that tickle, they zoom with glee,
Brightening the night, just wait and see!
They play hide and seek in the stellar sea,
A cosmic game of mirth and spree.

Cosmic Cabaret

Under the stars, they twirl and sway,
With socks on their heads, they dance all day.
Asteroids cheer with a raucous roar,
While planets giggle and beg for more.

Comets shoot pies through the darkened space,
Juggling moons with a wild, silly grace.
Black holes wink with a radiant shine,
In this cabaret of the cosmic divine.

Whimsical Warp Drives

Zooming through space on a whimsy ride,
Silly hats spinning, we can't help but glide.
Warp drives jolt with unpredictable glee,
As we tickle the stars just to see them flee.

Galaxies giggle as we twist and twirl,
Gravity dances, gives physics a whirl.
With every loop, laughter fills the void,
In this joyful ride, no fun is avoided.

Jovian Jests

Jupiter chuckles with a jovial grin,
As Saturn dons rings made of cotton and tin.
Mirth drips like nectar from Venusian hills,
Where laughter erupts and everyone thrills.

Meteors crack jokes in a fiery flight,
While aliens chuckle at the cosmic sight.
Eclipses wink, mischievous and spry,
In the court of the stars, the punchlines fly.

Infinity's Irony

In the depths of space where time takes a break,
Silly things happen, like stars that shake.
Quantum confetti bursts into play,
In an ironic twist, night dresses like day.

Lightyears away, laughter echoes loud,
As universes joke before the proud crowd.
Infinity teases with giggles and quirks,
In this cosmic realm where humor works.

Galactic Glee

In the void, stars wink and jest,
Cosmic giggles rising from the West.
Planets twirl in a silly dance,
While comets tease in their wild prance.

A moonbeam slips, a star goes 'pop',
Saturn's rings make all the jaws drop.
While aliens chuckle, watching the sight,
They laugh at our worries, oh what a delight!

Asteroids tumble like clumsy rhymes,
Jokes echo through the vast space climes.
Quasars blink with a knowing smile,
In this vastness, laughter stretches a mile.

So let's toast to the cosmic cheer,
For laughter floats in the atmosphere.
In the galaxy's embrace, we'll find,
A world where funny rules mankind.

Quantum Chuckles

In a realm where particles play,
Tiny whispers tickle the day.
Electrons dance a quirky jig,
While photons giggle, oh so big!

A wave of laughter, it seems to split,
Quantum quirks keep us all lit.
In the chaos, humor spins light,
With every quirk, the mood feels right.

Entangled jokes that loop and weave,
Enticing us all to just believe.
In the uncertainty of what's around,
The best of punchlines can always be found.

So let's harness the quirks we see,
In this strange world of harmony.
For every snicker reveals a truth,
That laughter lives on, ageless in youth.

Stardust Snickers

From nebulae, soft giggles flow,
As stardust twinkles with that special glow.
Shooting stars blink, sharing a grin,
While galaxies swirl, let the fun begin!

Cosmic tales whispered by the sun,
Of extraterrestrial pranks, oh what fun!
Dark matter chuckles, hiding its face,
In this vast universe, humor finds space.

Supernovae burst in brilliant cheer,
Painting the cosmos with laughter dear.
Astrological antics make us glee,
A sky full of punchlines, wild and free.

So when you gaze at the night so bright,
Remember the laughter that dances in light.
For in every star, a joke will reside,
Just sit back and enjoy the cosmic ride.

Black Hole Belly Laughs

Near the edge, where gravity sings,
A black hole chuckles, the joy it brings.
Swallowing laughter, it giggles wide,
As light itself tries to take a ride.

Spinning tales of things that cease,
It's the universe's own comic fleece.
What gets lost in its funny embrace,
Is just more laughter, a jolly space.

With every swirl, a punchline glows,
And spacetime bends, as humor flows.
Beyond the horizon, where all seems lost,
Comedic wonders come at no cost.

So next time you ponder the great unknown,
Remember that laughter can never be sown.
In the depths of the cosmos, we find our mirth,
Even where light vanishes, joy has its berth.

Celestial Comedy

Stars twinkle in a jolly dance,
Black holes play hide and seek with a glance.
Planets strike poses, all in a line,
Comets zip by, yelling, 'Isn't this fine?'

Galaxies giggle, swirling in jest,
While moons pull tides, giving planets a rest.
Asteroids tumble, a clumsy parade,
Creating a ruckus that won't soon fade.

Jovial Nebulas

Nebulas puff like cotton candy skies,
Colorful bursts that tickle the eyes.
Dust bunnies dance in a stellar waltz,
While cosmic winds add to the chaos.

Stars crack jokes in their luminous glow,
As meteors whiz past, putting on a show.
Laughter erupts in the vast, dark space,
With echoes of giggles all over the place.

Orbiting Laughter

Satellites circle, a merry-go-round,
With playful banter that's joyfully sound.
Rings of Saturn, a whimsical crown,
Each orbit brings laughter, never a frown.

The Milky Way spills its secrets of glee,
In a cosmic game of hide-and-seek spree.
Wormholes wink with a mischievous grin,
Pulling us in for a spin and a spin.

Cosmic Conundrums

Puzzles unfold in the space-time realm,
With quirky quirks that overwhelm.
Light-years tickle our funny bone,
In the depths of the void, we're never alone.

Quantum antics keep us perplexed,
As we giggle at how the universe flexed.
Gravity's riddle, a baffling sound,
Making us chuckle at all that we've found.

The Serendipity of Satire

In the realm where jesters dance,
Laughter spins in a wild prance.
Wit floats high, like birds in flight,
Chasing shadows in the light.

A tickle here, a giggle there,
Truth pokes fun with crafty flair.
Chortles travel through the air,
A grand parade of chuckles rare.

With jabs and jests, we play our game,
No two laughs are ever the same.
The punchlines bloom like springtime flowers,
Filling hearts in comical hours.

So raise a glass to humor's call,
In this cosmic jest, we stand tall.
For in the laughter, we align,
Finding joy in every line.

Laughter's Attraction

An echo bounces off the walls,
As giggles dance like bouncing balls.
With every chuckle, gravity bends,
Pulling together all our friends.

In playful splashes, we collide,
Like comets with laughter as our guide.
A merry jig in the starry night,
Attracting joy, a simple delight.

Beneath the moon's enchanting glow,
Our spirits lift, and faces glow.
With every joke, we're drawn much near,
A constellation of cheer, my dear.

So let this night be filled with glee,
In every smile, a jubilee.
For laughter's pull is ever strong,
In this grand dance, we all belong.

Humor in the Void

In the emptiness, there lies a grin,
A wink that says, 'Let the fun begin!'
Stars chuckle in the void so wide,
As we float on laughter's tide.

With cosmic jests that fly like comets,
Publishing hilarity like shared sonnets.
We're silly astronauts on quests of glee,
Surfing waves of pure jubilee.

In the silence, jokes take flight,
Black holes can't hide our delight.
Galaxies spin in fits of laughter,
Echoing joy here and hereafter.

Through the emptiness, we find our way,
Fueling smiles with every play.
For in this void, our values gleam,
On a ship of humor, we all dream.

Spheres of Joy

Rolling in circles, energies flow,
Laughter bounces, stealing the show.
Round and round, we giggle and spin,
Joy's embrace is where we begin.

Orbiting round in a cosmic dance,
Every chuckle gives chance a glance.
With each sphere, another snicker fades,
As the universe hums with light cascades.

In this playground of curves and spheres,
We weave our tales of hopes and fears.
A jolly swirl we all can share,
In the laughter's grip, we find our care.

So gather close, invite the cheer,
In joyous circles, we disappear.
For every jest brings another light,
In this world of joy, our spirits take flight.

Celestial Chuckles

A comet sneezed, stars did sway,
Pluto laughed, it's just play.
The moon wore a silly hat,
And danced with a friendly cat.

Asteroids rolled in joyful cheer,
Jupiter's belt shone so sheer.
A space whale sang a strange tune,
As Mars juggled with a balloon.

Saturn's rings tickled with flair,
Uranus giggled, who would dare?
Neptune spun, all in delight,
Tickling comets with pure light.

Galaxies twirled in a waltz,
Stars chuckled, "It's all our faults!"
With laughter echoing afar,
The universe, one big bizarre.

Whimsical Orbits

Planets prance in funny lines,
Venus wears socks with designs.
Mars flips over in a spin,
While Earth grins, "Let's begin!"

Satellites wink with a jest,
In this dance, they all invest.
Nebulas swirl in a haze,
Creating a cosmic maze.

Asteroids trot like clumsy fools,
While black holes bend all the rules.
Stars high-five in the night,
Shimmering with pure delight.

The cosmos jokes with a sigh,
As comets zoom and then fly.
Each orbit spins tales untold,
Of laughter in the vast, bold.

Laughter Among the Stars

A star had too much to drink,
And giggled until it turned pink.
With a wink it twirled around,
Making chuckles, a merry sound.

A dwarf planet gave a quick wink,
Saying, "Who says I can't think?"
Black holes fall into a fit,
A cosmic laugh, they can't quit.

Meteor showers bring the fun,
As asteroids race, on the run.
Galactic winds sweep across bright,
Filling space with sheer delight.

Echoes of joy stretch far and wide,
Among the stars, there's no need to hide.
With every laugh, the universe glows,
In a dance where joy always flows.

Cosmic Jests

A space-time riddle played in jest,
Where quarks giggle, feeling blessed.
Galaxies clash in comic play,
Creating new jokes every day.

Supernovae burst with surprise,
As they light up the midnight skies.
Planets spin, their tales do gleam,
In a cosmic pulsing dream.

Starlight twinkles with a grin,
As the universe, weaves within.
Gravity pulls, yet humor reigns,
In this dance, joy never wanes.

Orbits twist in merry loops,
As laughter binds the brightest troops.
Cosmic sounds ring out in glee,
From black holes to infinity.

Laughter Among the Stars

In space where silliness takes flight,
Asteroids giggle in the night.
Comets sneeze and twirl around,
As echoes of chuckles abound.

Gravity plays tricks on the moon,
Dancing shadows, a cosmic tune.
Planets wobble with glee in their spin,
For who can resist such a cosmic grin?

Meteorites start a tickle fight,
Juvenile pranks spark sheer delight.
In this vast expanse, joy's a must,
Stardust laughter turns into trust.

So let's frolic among the spheres,
Tickling the void, shedding our fears.
When spacetime bends, we'll laugh all the more,
Together in jokes, forever we soar.

The Universe Smiles

Galaxies wink with cheerful rays,
Lightyears away, they play and blaze.
Stars throw jokes like shooting lights,
In cosmic bars, they share their sights.

Astrophysics has a playful side,
With gravity's pull, they take a ride.
Laugh lines twinkle on each bright face,
As humor dances in endless space.

Black holes yawn, then swallow their pride,
Finding joy in the dark, they slide.
Supernovae burst with a riotous cheer,
Whispers of laughter resonate near.

Join the fun in this starlit spree,
Where the cosmos jiggles with glee.
In the expanse, we find our place,
Under the vast, embracing space.

Nebular Nonsense

In clouds of gas, where colors collide,
Giggling nebulae dance with pride.
Swirling patterns like tickling fingers,
Giving birth to stars that linger.

Wormholes wink with a playful muse,
Bending time in zany ruse.
Each twist elicits a comical sigh,
As space-time tickles, we can't deny.

Astronomers chuckle at distant sights,
Charting laughter through cosmic nights.
Silly theories twirl in delight,
As comets race in their joyful flight.

So we ponder the jokers of the skies,
Wondering how they keep their guise.
In the grand design, absurdity reigns,
As laughter above us never wanes.

Quasar Quips

Quasars beam with a radiant grin,
Bright as laughter that chases chagrin.
With punchlines that echo across the night,
Tickling the void with beaming light.

Whirling in chaos, they make us giggle,
As dark matter plays its cosmic wiggle.
In this comedy of vastness and flair,
Every light-year spreads joy in the air.

Twinkle, twinkle, oh boastful star,
Sharing secrets from afar.
Gravity's jokes leave us bemused,
In this universe, forever amused.

With telescopes pointed, humor in sight,
We laugh with the cosmos, basking in light.
So let us orbit round funny delights,
As we revel in quips through our nights.

Celestial Silliness

In space where the stars throw a dance,
A comet trips in a cosmic prance.
Planets wobble, giggling real loud,
As asteroids roll through a jovial crowd.

Nebulas puff with a cheeky grin,
While light-years echo with laughter within.
Quasars crack jokes in a bright, wild show,
Even the black holes can't help but glow.

The universe chuckles, a brilliant jest,
As moonbeams twinkle, giving their best.
Gravity's pulling a prank on us all,
Floating in whimsy, we heed the call.

With each starburst, we can't help but cheer,
As Martians drop pies, with a splash and a smear.
Through space we tumble, in joy we'll be lost,
In this cosmic comedy, we pay no cost.

Celestial Belly Laughs

Shooting stars zip in a belly flop,
Laughing as comets go 'kerplop'.
Galaxies spin in a playful swirl,
While asteroids giggle and twirl.

Space-time tickles, what a grand tease!
Black holes try to catch the breeze.
Stars toss confetti, light up the night,
With belly laughs bursting, oh what a sight!

On Jupiter's moons, they hold a fair,
With games and laughter filling the air.
Saturn's rings jingle with silly tunes,
As craters echo with playful balloons.

With a wink, the Milky Way plays a joke,
Sending a rocket flying, oh how it broke!
In this stellar circus, joy never ends,
In cosmic elation, we float with our friends.

Antigravity Amusements

Round and round, planets giggle and glide,
Gravity's lost in this zany ride.
Uranus smirks with its tilted pose,
While Mars wears a tutu, with flashy toes.

Comets make faces, zoom through a loop,
And asteroids dance in a merry troop.
Saturn spins tales with its sparkling rings,
As jovial sprites flap their luminous wings.

Nebulae bloom like candy floss,
In a swirl of colors, they laugh and toss.
Space is a carnival, nothing is stern,
With jokes on the solar wind's playful churn.

With each twist of fate, we float and we play,
In this whimsical realm, come join the fray.
A universe tickled, won't ever relent,
In boundless joy, our laughter is spent.

Cosmic Giggles

In the cosmic kitchen, stars bake a pie,
Asteroids taste it, and then they all cry!
With whipped cream comets, they laugh till they drop,
In the Milky Way's laughter, they can't seem to stop.

The sun cracks a pun, shining so bright,
As shadows giggle, slipping out of sight.
With twinkling jokes, the stars gather round,
Jupiter hiccups, a glorious sound.

Solar flares jump like a kid on a swing,
While meteors sing of a cheerful fling.
Space's embrace fills us with glee,
As laughter binds us, eternally free.

From moonlit pranks to celestial cheer,
Each twinkle of light calls us to draw near.
In the vastness of time, we join in the play,
Where cosmic giggles chase worries away.

Gravity-Less Grins

In a world where pies can fly,
A banana peel makes you sigh.
Cats in capes, they leap and bound,
Dancing on air, they're joyfully found.

Balloons that tickle the skies above,
Chasing the wind, they twist and shove.
Laughter erupts like soda streams,
In this lighthearted realm of dreams.

Juggling frogs with top hats keen,
Floating on clouds, it's all quite the scene!
Giggling gnomes at the garden gate,
Spreading cheer, oh isn't it great?

So let us embrace the foolish plight,
Where joy takes wing in pure delight!
Life's a circus, come take a spin,
Enjoy the ride, let the fun begin!

Celestial Comedy Hour

Stars wear glasses, what a sight!
Comets dancing in the night.
With slapstick rockets zooming around,
They tickle the moon without a sound.

Aliens burst in a belly laugh,
Telling jokes on the cosmic path.
Asteroids juggling in perfect sync,
Floating on laughter's joyful brink.

Supernovae make grand exits,
With confetti fizz and goofy fits.
Planets spin in a merry spree,
In this zany cosmic jubilee!

Grab your popcorn, the show is hot,
Catch the punchline, or you might get caught.
In this event, all are invited,
For humor in space, is truly ignited!

Orbiting Laughs

Planets pirouette, what a scene,
With rings of laughter, bright and keen.
In the orbit of giggles that swell,
Every motion tells a tale to tell.

Asteroids crack jokes, oh what a tease,
As they whiz by with such great ease.
The sun winks cheekily, full of mirth,
Warm rays of humor bouncing on earth.

Saturn's rings play a game of spin,
As Martians draw mustaches on the thin.
Jovian jesters jump with glee,
Making the universe chuckle in spree!

They tumble and twirl, in cosmic embrace,
In this joyful frenzy, there's plenty of space.
So join the ride on this giggle-filled path,
Where joy's the expectation, not just a laugh!

The Infinite Jest

A cosmic clown with oversized shoes,
Tripping on stars, spreading the news.
Galaxies chuckle, they sparkle and shine,
In the vast tapestry of playful design.

Silly satellites dance in pairs,
Doing cartwheels through the solar flares.
A wobbly spaceship blinks with delight,
Creating humor in the deep of night.

The universe chuckles at our tiny woes,
As it swirls and whirls with infinite flows.
Every laugh echoes in the void so wide,
Spreading joy on this silly ride.

So let's embrace the humor and jest,
In a world of wonders, we're truly blessed!
With each giggle that rings in the air,
We find our laughter everywhere!

Gravity's Giggle

In the dance of stars so bright,
Planets spin with sheer delight.
Comets slide on paths absurd,
Twirling like they've never heard.

Asteroids wearing silly hats,
Joking 'bout the cosmic spats.
Space-time bends to hear the jest,
As laughter travels, never rests.

Laughter Across Lightyears

Lightyears stretch like happy puns,
Echoing through the solar runs.
Saturn's rings, a merry swirl,
While Pluto claims its quirky pearl.

Stars exchange their cheeky winks,
In this void, no one thinks.
Galaxies giggle, dance, and play,
Brightening the vast array.

Cosmic Chuckles

Black holes whisper silly tales,
As stardust travels, tickled trails.
Nebulas puff with jovial pride,
Spreading joys from side to side.

The universe, a jester grand,
Pranks of space that never land.
Floating jokes in binary code,
Creating laughs along the road.

Celestial Antics

A moonbeam slips upon a star,
Chasing comets, oh so far.
The sun throws shade on a passing quark,
While meteors make sparks in the dark.

Galactic giggles rise and fall,
As quasars beam their playful call.
In this vast, amusing spree,
Joyful chaos, wild and free.

Space-Time Tickles

In the realm of stars that blink,
Wormholes dance and planets wink.
Galaxies swirl in cosmic glee,
A universe bursting, wild and free.

Asteroids joke, they roll and spin,
Comets burst forth with a cheeky grin.
Black holes laugh, they tug and pull,
Swirling humor, powerful and full.

Nebulas giggle in colors bright,
Whispering secrets in the night.
Stardust sprinkles, a playful show,
Laughter echoing, down below.

Light from the sun plays peek-a-boo,
With beams of joy, it shines anew.
In this vast playground of cosmic fun,
Every twinkle sings, "We've just begun!"

Lightyear Laughs

Zooming through space, a joke in flight,
Stars explode in shimmer and light.
Planets giggle as they go round,
While little moons just bounce, unbound.

A rocket ship laughs with engine roar,
Tickling the void and begging for more.
Cosmic balloons float in the breeze,
Jokes on the comets, teasing with ease.

Wormholes warp with a silly grace,
Slingshotting laughter across the space.
Each quasar twinkles with cheeky delight,
Spreading joy at the speed of light.

Across the cosmos, chuckles grow,
As starlit buddies put on a show.
In a universe brimming with cheer,
Space-time erupts, let's all draw near!

Comet's Comedic Journey

A comet's tail thrashes in play,
Juggling stardust all the way.
It zips by with a whoosh and a wink,
Sending sunbeams to the brink.

With each loop, a punchline's found,
In cosmic silences, laughter's profound.
Dust bunnies giggle in solar streams,
Chasing the comet, caught in dreams.

Twinkling lights in a dark expanse,
Galactic giggles invite the dance.
Through the void, a playful sight,
Spinning tales of pure delight.

As it travels, humorous spins,
Wobbling orbits, a chorus begins.
The galaxy's jesters, cheeky and bright,
Leave a trail of joy in the night!

Supernova Smiles

Bursting forth with a vibrant glow,
A star explodes, putting on a show.
Cheeky shadows that twist and play,
In the aftermath, laughter's sway.

Supernova sparks, igniting the cheer,
Cosmic confetti that tickles the ear.
Galaxies swirl in a jubilant jig,
Every twinkle sways, every gig a gig.

From the ashes, the humor spreads,
Funny little planets with silly threads.
Caught in a whirl of stellar jest,
This universe laughs, it's the very best.

So dance among the stars so bright,
Embrace the chaos of cosmic delight.
In heavenly bodies, joy intertwines,
As laughter echoes through the pines!

Jovial Pulls

In a world where silliness reigns,
Balloons float high, like comical trains.
Tickling toes with joyous delight,
We laugh as we drift, oh what a sight!

A hold on humor, we twist and twirl,
With each silly jest, our laughter can swirl.
Weightless giggles fly through the air,
Bringing smiles to faces, everywhere!

With puns that bounce like balls in a game,
Our joy takes flight, never feeling the same.
Dancing through moments, we'll never grow old,
In this coalition of laughter, we're bold!

So gather your friends, don't miss the fun,
For merriment shines like a bright rising sun.
To the rhythm of chuckles, we sway and we spin,
In this joyful galaxy, let the laughter begin!

The Weight of Laughter

When heavy hearts flip into a glee,
We juggle our woes, set them free.
A chuckle sneaks in like a thief in the night,
Transforming our burdens into sheer light.

With each hearty snort, the cosmos aligns,
Tumbling through banter, all quirks intertwine.
The scales tip with joy, tipping the mood,
As humor erupts like a bubbling brood!

From quips about clowns to tales of mishaps,
We weigh our laughs, then drop the false maps.
Floating on humor, we glide through the haze,
In this absurd universe, we spend our days.

The giggles we harvest, we hoard and we share,
With a wink and a nudge, joy's always there.
Amidst all the heaviness, laughter's the key,
Unlocking the heart with wild, silly glee!

Orbiting Smiles

In circles of cheer, we whirl and spin,
Our smiles catch light, where do we begin?
Gravity's pull? More like a tug on our face,
With each gleeful grin, there's no need for space.

A dance with the chuckles, free from restraint,
We leap through the air like a colorful paint.
Galaxies giggle, as we float all around,
Creating a cosmos of joy that we've found.

Whirling in laughter, we chase after stars,
With whimsy and wit, we travel so far.
No need for a rocket, just humor's embrace,
As we orbit through fun at a playful pace.

So gather your crew, let the laughter ignite,
With smiles as our fuel, we'll shine ever bright.
Through the vastness of joy, our hearts will take flight,
In this stellar adventure, we'll laugh through the night!

Laughter's Leap

With a leap and a bound, we jump with delight,
Soaring through giggles, oh what a sight!
Springing like bunnies from one punchline to next,
With joy in our hearts, we're truly perplexed.

The ground is but laughing, it urges our rise,
Tickles and chuckles, a feast for the eyes.
We pivot through puns with each jest and tease,
Laughter's our trampoline, it's sure to please.

As gravity loosens its firm, heavy grip,
We flip and we twirl, like a whimsical trip.
In mid-air we capture the essence of fun,
With each hearty laugh, we're never outdone!

So come take a jump, don't hold back your mirth,
In the playground of joy, let's celebrate worth.
Through laughter's great leap, we'll rise to the skies,
Anchored with smiles, our spirits will fly!

Astounding Antics

In a world where bananas fly,
Monkeys giggle as they try.
Feet stuck in jelly, oh what a sight,
Laughter echoes into the night.

Juggling jellybeans on the moon,
See the space cat with a broom.
Silly space cows dance with glee,
Galloping sideways, oh so free.

Wobbling with every step they take,
A trampoline made of cake.
Slipping, sliding with squeals so bright,
Who knew the cosmos could be so light?

Aliens burst with fits of glee,
Tickled by stars, oh let it be!
Gravity laughs, it's all a game,
In this strange world with no shame.

The Lighthearted Leap

Bouncing high, they touch the sky,
Jelly shoes make them fly.
Laughter ripples through the crowd,
As every leap is wild and loud.

Twirling in a cosmic dance,
Floating free, they take a chance.
A silly hat on every head,
Making jokes no one would dread.

Stars chuckle as they wink and shine,
Blasting joy like fizzy wine.
Footloose in a comet's tail,
They giggle hard, they never fail.

Each twist and turn, a burst of fun,
Under the rays of a distant sun.
Gravity pulls, but they don't care,
In this lighthearted, endless air.

Hefty Humor in a Weightless World

In a realm where heaviness floats,
Laughter bounces off silly boats.
Tugs of war with squishy clouds,
Joyful shouts from happy crowds.

Doughnuts whirl in zero-G,
As spacemen dance with glee.
Giggles echo through the void,
Each moment filled, never destroyed.

A weighty joke that never lands,
Unicorns toss flowers in their hands.
Puns fly high, a cosmic treat,
No gravity can resist this beat.

Through cosmic fields, they streak and laugh,
In the fluffiest of paragraphs.
It's a riot beyond belief,
In a weightless world of pure relief.

Beyond the Event Horizon

Peeking past the boundary line,
Where giggles swirl and stars align.
Jumping past the black hole's edge,
Where every jest's a playful pledge.

Floating donuts roll with grace,
Prancing in the endless space.
Comets wearing funny hats,
Racing past oblivious cats.

Bouncing back from time so funny,
Chasing rays of light like honey.
With every twirl, they paint the night,
In colors bold and pure delight.

Beyond where silence can't confine,
Jokes arise like vintage wine.
In the vastness, laughter's found,
A universe of joy unbound.

www.ingramcontent.com/pod-product-compliance
Lightning Source LLC
Chambersburg PA
CBHW072148200426
43209CB00051B/842